AMELIA SAINT

G000168526

TABLE
DECORATING
BOOK

AMELIA SAINT GEORGE'S
TABLE DECORATING BOOK

WITH 8 PAGES OF PULL-OUT DESIGNS

PHOTOGRAPHS BY
JULIE FISHER

EBURY PRESS
LONDON

I should like to dedicate this book to my mother Barbara Poeton and my grandmother Daisy Bevis. Nana has, throughout my life, been on the other end of the phone to share joys or support my troubles. As children we often stayed, as have my children. Our first job was to lay the table looking out over the garden, and I thank her for all her help and friendship.

My mother has not always approved of my choices, however we have rarely disagreed on design, be it a table, dress, house or flowers. My mother's gift with flowers is demonstrated throughout this book, for which, along with most other teachings, I thank her.

First published 1995

1 3 5 7 9 10 8 6 4 2

Text copyright © Amelia Saint George 1995
Photographs copyright © Julie Fisher 1995

The right of Amelia Saint George to be identified as
the author of this book has been asserted by her in accordance
with the Copyright, Designs and Patents Act 1988.

First published in the United Kingdom in 1995 by Ebury Press,
Random House, 20 Vauxhall Bridge Road, London SW1V 2SA

Random House Australia (Pty) Limited
20 Alfred Street, Milsons Point, Sydney,
New South Wales 2061, Australia

Random House New Zealand Limited
18 Poland Road, Glenfield,
Auckland 10, New Zealand

Random House South Africa (Pty) Limited
PO Box 337, Bergvlei,
South Africa

Random House UK Limited Reg. No. 954009

A CIP catalogue record for this book is available from the British Library

ISBN 009 179046 8

Editor Emma Callery
Photographer Julie Fisher
Designer Paul Wood

Colour separations by Wace Corporate Imaging, London
Typeset from author's disk
Printed in Hong Kong by Sheck Wah Tong Printing Press Limited

Contents

Introduction

I have written this book on table decorating to show you ways to entertain your guests even before the meal has begun. Many of us lead busy lives and should like to give our friends and family more attention and find that sitting and eating at a relaxed and well decorated table is a great way to do just that.

I frequently make the decoration the food, and the food the decoration, which means that I can then stay at the table with my friends enjoying their company, rather than hopping up and down, changing plates and shuffling the food. Like most of us I enjoy eating food and socialising equally, and with a little forethought it really is possible to make entertaining an enjoyable experience.

In this book there are fourteen different themed table settings, each designed with a different time of the year in mind. Many of them feature decorations that you can simply cut straight from the middle of the book. There are, for instance, colourful napkin rings, menu cards and a lampshade. Similarly, in the stencil section I have provided you with stencil outlines for a star, some children's party animals and Christmas holly and mistletoe (see the instructions opposite for using the pull-out section).

In addition to the pull-out section, in this book there are many other interesting suggestions for simple things to make when decorating your tables. Cross stitch rose buds, templates for patchwork, a ginger-bread farm house and animal biscuits, and the most exquisite flower arrangements are but a selection of the projects that fill this book.

Do have a go — be as adventurous as I have. It was such fun filling the hollowed eggs with liquid chocolate, and making the scalloped tablecloth and cushions was equally simple and the end result so elegant. The découpage table mats give me great pleasure every time I use them — and do try making papier mâché bowls over balloons, the art is really very versatile.

My life is in this book, ranging as it does from weddings to small children's parties; or picnics on the beach and barbecues at dusk to lunch outside or harvest by the fireside. I very much hope it will become part of your life too.

USING THE PULL-OUT SECTION

1 Before cutting out or stencilling any of the decorations, remove the relevant page(s) from the centre of the book. Do this by cutting out the card pages as near to the middle of the book as possible. The tracing paper pages have perforations down the edge so that you can pull out the pages as you need them.

2 To use the cardboard table decorations, cut around the outline with either small, sharp embroidery scissors or use a craft knife on a cutting mat. Make the decorations as described in the book.

3 To use any of the stencils, take out the tracing paper pages and make the designs into stencils as described on page 8. If you decide that you would like to alter the size of any of the stencils, enlarge or reduce them on a photocopier and then follow the instructions on page 8.

These vegetable etchings are featured in the pull-out section on page 54. Detailed making instructions are given on page 73.

BASICS

The following step-by-step sequences show you exactly how to do the core techniques that are featured in this book. In each one I list what materials and equipment you will need and then take you through the technique offering advice on the best way to tackle things, and the pitfalls to avoid. Once you are armed with these skills, you will be able to decorate any table most successfully.

STENCILLING

Stencilling is so versatile; once you have cut out your design you can use it whole, or just part of it, turn it upside down, flip it over to reverse it, change your colours at will — in fact, almost anything. On pages 45-51 of this book, there are numerous tracing paper stencils for you to use (see page 7 on how to use them), and just in case you should feel like creating your own or altering the size of a stencil given in this book (just use a photocopier to enlarge or decrease the size), here is my advice on cutting out and stippling.

The holly leaves and mistletoe stencil put into practice. There are very many different ways to use a stencil once you have prepared it.

WHAT YOU WILL NEED

Tracing or parchment paper

Soft pencil

Oiled manila stencil paper

Cutting knife and mat

Fabric

Masking tape

Fabric paints

Stencil brush

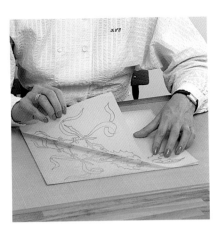

1 Oiled manila stencil paper is the best medium to use for making stencils as it keeps its shape well and the cut lines remain crisp. To transfer a design onto manila paper, use the tracing paper outlines in the centre of the book, or trace the design of your choice onto tracing or parchment paper, and go over the back of it with a soft pencil. Place the tracing paper onto the manila paper and draw over the lines of the design one more time with the pencil and then lift off the tracing paper. The outline should then be transferred to the manila (see above). If necessary, make the lines darker with the pencil.

2 Using the cutting knife and mat, cut out the stencil details. Here (above) I am using the holly leaves and mistletoe stencil featured on pages 82-7, so I am cutting out the leaves, stalks, berries and ribbon bit by bit. Always cut holding the manila paper firmly with one hand. Continually alter the position of your supporting hand as the blade carves out the leaves as it should never be in line with your hand in case it slips. If you are worried about using a knife such as this, use nail scissors. It takes a little longer but works equally well.

3 Position the stencil on the surface you are going to decorate. You might find it useful to hold the stencil in place with masking tape — if you are working on a table it might be necessary, but on small, shaped surfaces or on walls it certainly will be. Then set to work with the brush and paint, stippling with a light tapping motion onto the fabric (see above). Use a small amount of paint at a time, building it up gently as it cannot be removed once it becomes too dark. Here I have tipped some of the paint into the lids of the paint pots but you could just as easily use saucers or lids of disused plastic containers.

4 I chose to stencil the napkins first using only a part of the design. As I knew this in advance I only cut out this part of the stencil. However, if the whole stencil had been cut I could just as easily have used masking tape to cover the parts of the stencil that I didn't want to use. In this way you can make your stencil incredibly versatile.

5 However, on the place mat (see page 86), I used the whole stencil. Once you are happy with your stippling and feel that the colours couldn't be improved, just lift off the manila paper to reveal the stencil beneath (see left). Iron your work on the reverse side with a dry iron for several minutes to the tolerance of the fabric and then it is fully washable. Equally, if you have made a mistake, do not iron it and the paint will come out in subsequent washes.

MAKING PAPIER MACHE BOWLS

Using lining wallpaper for making these papier mâché bowls is ideal. They become strong enough to use after three to four layers and the cream finish is also most conducive to all paint treatments. However, experiment with other papers too as they can be such fun — any wrapping paper, tissue paper, sweet wrappers, silver foil, brown paper will do. The list is endless and it is all waiting to be played with. If you want to leave your work half-finished, cover it temporarily with plastic wrap.

WHAT YOU WILL NEED

Lining wallpaper

Strong wallpaper paste

Balloons

Bowl

PVA adhesive

Varnish

1 Neatly rip up the lining paper into small pieces. Experiment with tearing across the paper and up and down — you will find that it will tear into strips more neatly one way than the other. For small balloons, make smaller pieces of paper. The pieces should overlap on the surface of the balloon and they must lie flat and neither buckle nor stick out.

2 Blow up a balloon and wet the surface. Stand the balloon in a bowl. Taking the bits of paper piece by piece, soak them in the wallpaper paste and then stick them on to the balloon (see right). Begin at the top and radiate outwards and downwards, overlapping the papers neatly. This will give excellent coverage. Work to the depth of the balloon that you want your finished bowl to be. and leave the paper to dry.

3 To achieve a strong and even bowl, add a second layer of glued paper, this time placing the strips around the bowl rather than placing them up and down (see below). Descend to the same level as before . Repeat steps 2 and 3 until you are happy that the bowl is strong enough.

4 Cover the bowl completely with a layer of PVA adhesive which acts as a sealant and strengthener. It is transparent when dry. When completely dry, either burst or eàse the balloon out of the bowl. It will come clean away (see below). Then paint the inside of the bowl with the PVA and leave to dry overnight.

5 You can decorate these bowls in any way you like (see below). I used gold leaf for New Year (see page 17), paint for Easter (see page 27), and découpage for a summer lunch (see page 72). Acrylic paints are really easy to apply and followed by a few layers of varnish for protection, the bowls are lightly waterproof. I use mine for salads, fruits and bread, but nothing resting in water. Wash them with soapy water, but don't use an abrasive cleaner and never immerse in water.

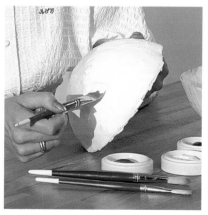

DECOUPAGE

The gluing and sticking that we all did as children can totally transform place mats, trays, tables, and even whole walls. Découpage, the craft of sticking paper pictures onto a surface, is very simple and any images can be used. In this book, for example, I have used photographs beneath a transparent plastic tray (see page 24), and colourful vegetables on a table to eat off outside (see page 71), and etchings on a dining room wall and table setting (see pages 79). Cut images out of magazines, sketch books, cartoons, cards — anything can be used for this delightfully easy form of decoration.

WHAT YOU WILL NEED

Images

Cutting knife and mat

PVA adhesive

Varnish

1 Gather or photocopy as many images as you require for the object you are covering with découpage. Here I am decorating some table mats and I have decided to repeat the same image around the edge, so lots of photocopies are needed. Should you want to vary the sizes of your images, reduce or enlarge them on a photocopier to appropriate sizes.

2 Cut out the images using the cutting knife and mat (see above). Always cut holding the paper firmly with one hand. Continually alter the position of your supporting hand as the blade carves out the images. It should never be in line with your hand in case it slips. If you are worried about using a knife such as this, use nail scissors. It takes a little longer but works equally well.

3 If you want to continue a design in long strips, lay one découpage piece over another, moving them about until they work well together. Cut the pieces accordingly. You might also decide to remove other details or bits of background — it is really easy to do this, making découpage a very flexible craft. For example, on this table mat I decided to cut away the background between the twisting ribbons and the rod so that more of the mat would show through (see above).

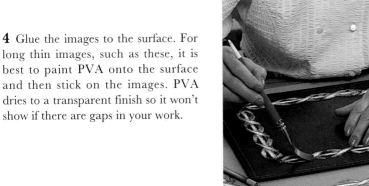

4 Glue the images to the surface. For long thin images, such as these, it is best to paint PVA onto the surface and then stick on the images. PVA dries to a transparent finish so it won't show if there are gaps in your work.

5 Seal the découpage with an additional layer of PVA over the top (see left) and when it is completely dry protect it with several layers of heat and water resistant varnish. If your object has been finished in this way, it can be washed with soapy water, but don't use an abrasive cleaner on it and never immerse it in water .

FLOWER ARRANGING

Whole books are devoted to flower arranging, but as the arrangement featured on page 59 is so pretty and easy to make I thought it would be lovely to show you how to make it. It could be used for all sorts of occasions throughout the year, making any table setting very special. To make the stand for this arrangement, I attached a small receptacle to the top of a silver candlestick.

WHAT YOU WILL NEED

Receptacle

Florist's foam

Sharp knife

Florist's tape (optional)

Candlestick

Candle

Flowers (eg, freesias, roses, narcissus)

Trailing greenery (eg, ivy, clematis, winter jasmine)

1 Place the receptacle upside down over the florist's foam and mark where you will need to cut the foam so that it fits snugly without allowing movement. Cut the foam (see below) and position it in the receptacle. If necessary, secure it with florist's tape.

2 Submerge the foam and the receptacle in water and leave for about 15 minutes until all the air bubbles have stopped coming out of it. Place the candle firmly into the oasis and then put the receptacle onto the candlestick. Now you can start arranging your greenery. As this container is tall, it invites fine trailing greenery, so place one long trail on either side of the candle, reserving other strands for later filling.

3 Place four roses so that they fan out with two on either side of the candle (see below). Frequently, successful flower arrangements have three, five or seven flowers placed together; here the candle makes the fifth 'flower' in this arrangement.

4 Put freesias between the roses (see right). Add more flowers in front of the candle, fanning them out equally, as before. Then step back from your arrangement and see if there are any naked spots. If so, fill these in with greenery.

5 To make sure that your arrangement will last as long as possible, spray it with water and keep in a cool place overnight. Top up the oasis frequently with water — flowers drink a lot.

MAKING A TOPIARY TREE

These trees are elegant and can be used for various occasions as they can bear different crops, ranging from sweets for a children's party or Christening, to Christmas decorations or lovely dried flowers. On pages 32-3 a topiary tree covered with tomato and spinach is featured, and here are step-by-step instructions for making it.

WHAT YOU WILL NEED

Florist's foam sphere

Plastic wrap

3 bamboo canes

Earth or hobby cement

Flower pot or similar receptacle

Moss

Cocktail sticks

Baby tomatoes

Spinach leaves

1 Florist's foam spheres are available in various sizes-this one has a diameter of 20cm (8in). Because food will be used to cover this sphere, cover it with plastic wrap, tucking the ends into the base (see above).

2 Holding the three bamboo canes together, force them centrally into the sphere by about 10cm (4in) (see above). Mark the bamboo if you aren't happy to judge this distance by eye. The sphere will then sit firmly on the bamboo trunk.

3 Fill the flower pot with earth (for a larger arrangement, cement might be appropriate) compacting it firmly. Then plunge the trunk into the earth. When deciding how tall you want your tree to be, remember that quite a lot of the trunk will disappear into the pot. Don't make it too tall, however, as the tree will then topple over fairly easily. Cover the earth with moss to make it look more attractive.

4 To cover the sphere, spear each baby tomato with a cocktail stick and poke the other end into the sphere (see right). For variety, I added baby spinach leaves around some of the tomatoes; mainly those on the lower part. Build up the tomatoes uniformly until you have totally covered the surface. Don't stick tomatoes here and there only — the tree will look somewhat moth eaten. Spray the tree with a light mist of water and leave it in a cool place before eating.

NEW YEAR'S EVE

Taking gold and white as a theme for a dinner party on New Year's Eve is both unusual and sophisticated — crisp white linen with gold cutlery and gold stencilled stars is fresh and enticing. A can of gold spray paint is all that you need to add details to your tablecloth and napkins, and ribbons can also be used to enliven the soft furnishings.

Preparing the table for a dinner party requires little forethought — tablecloth, mats, coasters, cutlery, side plates, glasses and napkins are the essential ingredients. But to decorate the table so that it looks that little bit different, that little bit more exciting for the arrival of the new year, requires some advance planning. Take a theme, such as the gold stars featured here, and decorate any element you care to. I chose to decorate the tablecloth and napkins, but don't feel constrained to these items — how about continuing the star theme on menu and name cards if the party is a more formal occasion; or on candles and candlesticks, place mats and coasters? You might even choose to cut out stars from cardboard, spray them gold and suspend them from the ceiling above the dining table, making your very own Milky Way.

Ribbons can be particularly dramatic and another way to use ribbons on napkins can be found on page 80. Here I chose two contrasting gold ribbons to use as borders for the napkins and tablecloth. Ensure that you buy washable ribbons as they will require frequent washing. I describe in detail how to make these napkins overleaf.

The star stencil is featured in the tracing paper pull-out section in the middle of this book, and cutting stencils is described in detail on page 9. For a thematic party such as this one, you must remember to cut your stencil in a variety of sizes so use a photocopier to enlarge and reduce the outline provided here to suitable sizes. For the larger stars you may choose to create slightly more ornate ones. Use large stars on the tablecloth — perhaps interspersed with smaller ones; medium-sized outlines on the napkins, and small stars on the finer items such as candles and name cards.

THE PULL-OUTS

Star stencil on page 45

See page 7 for how to use the pull-out section

Using gold and white as a theme for decorating a New Year's Eve dinner party table can be great fun. This particular party giver is evidently continuing the present-giving tradition, and has stencilled gold stars on the wrapping paper.

Menu
• • •
Melon
• • •
Saumon
• • •
Gâteau

THE STENCILLED STARS

Stencilling is quick, easy and inexpensive, and on this tablecloth and napkins the stars look crisp and effective. Gold is difficult to find in fabric paints, so I have used gold spray paint which after numerous washes will fade. When this happens, you could either re-stencil the same stars or leave the fading ones as distant stars and stencil brighter stars in the galaxy.

WHAT YOU WILL NEED

Star stencil (page 45)

Cutting mat and knife

Repositionable spray glue

Spray paint (gold)

1 Remove the tracing pull-out from page 45 and make your stencil as outlined on page 9.

2 Before beginning to spray, make wide borders around the edge of the stencil from scrap paper to prevent the paint from spreading onto the surrounding surface.

3 Attach the stencil to the surface. It is best to use a repositionable spray glue on the back of the stencil as this will prevent the spray paint from pushing beneath the stencil, giving your star a slightly blurred edge. Alternatively, hold the stencil close to the fabric while spraying — but, beware, you will end up with very gold fingertips.

THE RIBBON NAPKINS AND TABLECLOTH

There are so many beautiful ribbons about, so treat yourself and try some. To edge the tablecloth and napkins, I used a combination of ribbons echoing the colours in the plates. I also bought a length of gold ribbon with wire stiffening from which I created the napkin rings. They really are quick and easy to make. Simply cut ribbon to the required length and tie around the corner of each napkin which has previously been folded into four — the end result is unusual and remarkably effective. The wire allows you to mould the ribbon into interesting shapes, and prevents it from falling limply on the side plate.

WHAT YOU WILL NEED

Ribbons (various)

Sewing machine

Cotton thread

1 To cover the edges of the napkins and tablecloth, fold each ribbon in half, press and baste over the napkin and tablecloth edges. If you choose to use more than one ribbon, baste on the wider one(s) first, followed by the narrower ones in succession.

2 Mitring can be very awkward and I find that overlapping the ribbons at the corners to make squares can be just as effective.

3 Machine stitch in place. Then fold under the ends and oversew to neaten.

THE PAPIER MACHE BOWLS

These bowls could use up the trailing balloons from festivities, and all the precious discarded wrapping papers. Experiment with papers when making the papier mâché as you can combine different thicknesses and textures to create some startling results. Tissue paper can be particularly effective as you can layer it on smoothly, or add texture by ruffling it up and then gluing it in place. Dutch metal leaf is a cheaper form of gold leaf and the end result is just as good. It is available from any good art shop.

WHAT YOU WILL NEED

Lining paper

Strong wallpaper paste

Balloons

Bowl

Acrylic gel medium

Sweet wrappers or Dutch metal leaf

Acrylic paints

Varnish

1 Make the bowls as described on page 10.

2 To achieve the gold sheen on these particular bowls, use fine sweet and chocolate wrappings peeled from their backings. Or if you are feeling adventurous, use Dutch metal leaf available at art shops. Paint on a thin layer of acrylic gel medium and then apply the metal leaf onto it. As you pull off the backing sheet, the leaf is left stuck to the adhesive. Leave to dry thoroughly.

3 Paint the bowls with several coats of varnish to protect them.

ST VALENTINE'S DAY

Creating an intimate dinner gives great pleasure and with forethought everything can be reused for different occasions. St Valentine dates from the third century and has no romantic setting in his martyrdom. However, birds are supposed to pair on 14 February and calling oneself a Valentine appears in Chaucer's letters. So romance is definitely in the air — and how better to further this than with a softly caressing toile de Jouy tablecloth, subdued lighting and roses, roses everywhere?

Create the mood by suggestion rather than force. The tablecloth, for example, is subtle and beautifully detailed. To me, the embracing couple and the man pulling his beloved on a swing evoke summers past and — hopefully — to come. But as they are in eighteenth-century dress, it is discreet with an innocent touch of having time to spare.

For an intimate dinner, lighting is most important so that you can relax and enjoy one another's company. The rose wreath centrepiece is illuminated by floating candles in the bowl to give a warm and kind light source. For other illumination in the room, I would suggest subdued, smaller lights. If you do not have a dimmer switch, keep a lower wattage bulb available.

In addition to being a light source, the rose wreath is a most unusual centrepiece in that the orange of the kumquats strikingly contrasts with the red toile de Jouy. Its success lies in the fact that it is the only piece of extravagance on an otherwise restrained table setting.

The scalloped napkin ring is featured on page 43. I have designed a more ornate version for the pull-out section for variety. It is repeated four times to allow for larger supper parties. Cut out as many of the rings as you require, cut along the dotted lines and slot them together. Should you want to recreate the napkin rings featured in the photograph opposite, transfer the outline on page 43 onto thin cardboard and hatch red lines around the scallops.

The table is set with strong blue under-plates contrasting with the tablecloth, whereas the inner dinner plates are calm and elegant and would suit most menus. Anything more heavily patterned might be far too distracting — especially with the colourful rose wreath — detracting from the quiet evening ahead.

THE PULL-OUTS

Napkin rings on page 43

See page 7 for how to use the pull-out section

Love is in the air. Champagne, roses and home-made chocolates — what better way would there be to celebrate St Valentine's day?

THE ROSE WREATH

Unfurl your love and be unabashed that you desire to make the effort for the one you love. Roses, of course, are essential, but how about adding some little kumquats for a dash of passion? Should you wish to leave the wreath to dry, leave it lying horizontally and it will dry within a week or two (depending on humidity). You may well need to tuck more moss into the sausage through the holes from underneath as everything will have dried and become looser. The flowers too will become smaller as they dry and so some gaps may appear in which case just pop another flower in — it will dry soon enough. Now that your wreath has a little more stuffing, you can hang it on the wall as a reminder of your evening.

WHAT YOU WILL NEED

Chicken wire

36 kumquats

24 roses

Moss

Orange kumquats, red roses and green moss surrounding floating candles create a striking and romantic centrepiece.

1 Take a sufficient length of chicken wire to fit around your bowl. Roll it up like a sausage, stuff it with moss and hang it over the bowl using wayward chicken wire strands at intervals to keep it in place.

2 Then wire your kumquats in pairs, or threes if you can manage it, and push them firmly into the moss. If, like me, you intend to keep your wreath, press the wires right through the wreath, bend them around a bit of chicken wire and conceal them back in the moss.

3 Cut the roses back to 6cm (2¹/₂in) stems and clump them in groups of three or five in the moss. Cut the stems as they reappear through the back of the wreath.

THE SCALLOPED NAPKINS

These napkins are very simple to make using satin stitch on a sewing machine but it might be worth having a few practice goes on some remnants before tackling the real thing. The end result is soft and flowing, and you can repeat the scallops on the edge of the tablecloth and chair cushion (see below).

WHAT YOU WILL NEED

Cotton or linen (white)

Sewing machine

Cotton thread (red)

1 Cut your chosen fabric to size (an averagely sized napkin is 30 sq cm [12 sq in]) and draw the scalloped edge around all four sides using a washable pen. Machine stitch along the line in your chosen colour.

2 Then, using a buttonhole tension so that the stitches neatly lie next to each other, begin to make the satin stitch scallops. At the top of each scallop, use the minimum width setting and as you stitch to the bottom of the scallop, gently ease your width setting to maximum. Slowly return to the minimum setting to finish the scallop.

The scalloped theme is continued with the napkin rings which are simply made from strips of cardboard slotted together to make circles.

3 Once you have finished the satin stitch scallops, very carefully remove the excess fabric around the outside using sharp embroidery scissors.

THE SCALLOPED TABLECLOTH AND CUSHION COVER

To continue the theme of scallops, I have chosen to add scallops around the edge of the square tablecloth and cushion cover - the pretty softness of the edges adds to the romance I feel. By making a sort of envelope for these items, I have employed a wonderfully simple technique to avoid having to overstitch along one of the edges.

WHAT YOU WILL NEED

Main fabric

Lining fabric

Sewing machine

Cotton thread

1 Cut two squares of material to the size you desire — the main fabric and a lining for the tablecloth, two pieces of main fabric for the cushion cover. Make the backing square 5cm (2in) larger all around and then cut it in half and place on the main fabric, right sides together, so that the selvedges of the backing overlap each other across the centre. Pin and baste the two layers together, 5cm (2in) in from the edge of the front piece of fabric.

2 To make the scallops, evenly position tea plates for the tablecloth and cups for the cushion cover along one edge of the fabric allowing 6mm (¼in) between each. Draw around the outside edge of each plate or cup to give you the scalloped edge outline. Repeat on each edge.

3 Stitch around the scalloped line, and trim the fabric close to the stitching, clipping Vs around the semi-circles to ease the fabric. Turn right sides out through the centre back opening and press. To finish the cushion, add a line of satin stitching within the scallops.

Scalloped edges for the napkins, tablecloth and cushion cover take the hard lines from these soft furnishings.

MOTHER'S DAY

Most of my memories of Mothering Sunday are of small children energetically arranging their present made at school onto a rather over-burdened tray. I became wiser as the years went by and everything was put at my children's height, especially anything in the fridge. Trying to pretend to be asleep, as they pushed open my bedroom door, amused them as much as me.

For this reverse découpage tray, we had great fun picking out the rejected photographs to form a lovely and very personal tray. It forms a record of my children's growth, holidays with grandparents and friends — all the most precious moments grouped together to give great pleasure for the year to come.

All those photographs that weren't deemed quite good enough to be put into an album had rather sadly been relegated to a large brown box and rarely delved into. Most of the pictures had been discarded because of the background, so using them for découpage was ideal, cutting away only the images that my children and I liked. We selected the best bits of their younger childhood, their grandparents, and even my little Goddaughter sucking her thumb. Details for making the tray are given overleaf but don't feel constrained to making reverse découpage on a tray like this alone. You could also use clear photograph frames or large glass plates. Indeed,

anything that is transparent is ideal and can be given a new lease of life with this fun and easy form of découpage.

The napkins folded as envelopes are an amusing detail (see page 91 for making instructions). Looking as though the post had just been delivered, one of the envelopes contained a hand-made Mother's Day card. I made a lino cut for this card, but you could choose to stencil, potato print, or paint a simple outline. It's the thought that counts.

The wonderful scented narcissus tied into a small posy and simply tied with a ribbon is a charming addition to this breakfast tray. It reflects the traditions of Mothering Sunday during the Industrial Revolution when many working children and domestic servants had little opportunity to see their parents. The Church then created Mothering Sunday on the second Sunday in March when the children gathered together any flowers that they could find and presented them to their mothers in church.

A fresh cup of cappuccino sprinkled with chocolate and warm croissants accompanied by a loving card and fresh bunch of flowers would delight any mother.

THE REVERSE DECOUPAGE TRAY

When you are choosing the photographs to stick on the back of this tray, find more than you think you will need, as you will be cutting away the background so making them smaller. I was amazed just how many photographs were needed to cover this tray — 24 in all. When I chose the pictures, I originally started with heads only as I thought they would be easy to cut, but in composing them I found it better to have a mixture of heads and bodies. I cut the photographs using a scalpel and cutting mat, but my daughters used sharp embroidery scissors. Give yourself scope when cutting. For example, there is a photograph of my son in his crib when newly born, and I chose to leave the crib in the photograph rather than cutting it out. However, had I needed a small image, I could then have cut him out of the crib too.

WHAT YOU WILL NEED

Clear plastic tray

Discarded photographs

Cutting mat and sharp knife or small embroidery scissors

Re-usable adhesive

Dry glue stick or spray glue

Fabric backing (gingham)

PVA glue

Paintbrush

Polyurethane varnish

1 Arrange your cut out photographs underneath the base of the tray, overlapping pictures here and there. Use small pieces of re-usable adhesive to keep them in place temporarily. If the tray has any ridges, just mould the photographs firmly over them. Once you are happy with the layout, use the dry glue stick or spray glue to stick the photographs down (don't use wet glue as it will disfigure your photographs). Work from the centre outwards and remove the re-usable adhesive blobs as you reach them.

2 Leave the glue to dry thoroughly and then take the backing fabric and lay it on the underside of the tray, over the photographs. Make sure the right side of the fabric is face down, so that you will see it from the top side of the tray once you have finished.

3 Don't cut the material, just paint on a layer of the PVA glue. It will filter through the material and onto the photographs but won't get them wet and make them buckle. Allow the glue to dry thoroughly (for several hours or overnight), and then paint on another coat. This time make the coat slightly thicker than before and pay particular attention to the edge of the tray. Leave once more overnight and then with a sharp knife, carefully slice the excess fabric away from the edge of the tray. The PVA will have sealed the edge and there should be no fraying.

4 Coat the base with several layers of polyurethane varnish and leave to dry. The tray is then ready for use. You can wipe over the tray as usual, but don't submerge it in water, otherwise you will have water babies!

THE ENVELOPE NAPKIN

This is such a charming folded napkin and I think it looks good on any breakfast or tea table setting. The instructions for folding it are on page 91.

THE POSY

Posies can be very elaborate, or equally very simple, such as this one here. Indeed, this one is so simple a child could make it which is, after all, the purpose of Mother's Day. Frequently when gathering flowers I use an elastic band to keep them together and then tuck different leaves into the layers of elastic for the simplest and most effective posy. To finish off a posy such as this, all one need do is then lightly wrap a ribbon over the elastic band and cut the stems neatly.

My reverse découpage tray features my family but you might prefer to cut out photographs of flowers, animals, or anything else that takes your fancy.

EASTER

As well as being a religious festival, Easter is a time of fun and folly with fantastic chocolates in every form being eaten around the world. One Easter I felt that I should rethink my celebrations and in place of buying all the plastic and cardboard packaging that eggs so frequently come in, I set to and experimented with filling my own eggs, making my own papier mâché bowls, and bought some recycled glass plates. During the year I also made a patchwork tablecloth out of men's shirts — and here is the result of all this labour.

Easter is a time to sit back and think a little and be fortified, whether it be by the religious implications of the time or by the season's new growth in the form of unfurling buds and longer days. It is a time to look to the future, and like many other people, I have become increasingly aware of how much we are all consuming. If I think back to my Grandmother's values, she lived through two world wars and 'made do' along with everyone else. This recycled table is neither dowdy nor humble, but apart from the raw ingredients, which were eaten, nothing was thrown away. Of all the tables in this book, this is the one that I most enjoyed — and it is the one that took the most time to create.

The tablecloth, for example, took many months of labour. The collecting together of so many men's shirts (all of which have been worn) is bound to cause amusement. However, many brave fellows contributed, so I have a wonderful record of my son, father, brothers and friends to form a fresh, three-dimensional look on life. The making instructions and templates are given on page 29.

The papier mâché bowls were also hand made and I chose to reflect the patchwork designs and swirling egg cups in the painted decorations around the rims. These plates and glasses are inexpensive and made of recycled glass.

I am the only woman in my family not driven by a craving for chocolate, but having smelled the melting chocolate being poured into the hollowed blown eggs, I can begin to understand the addiction (see overleaf for making instructions). The egg carton requires still more chocolate, and even more chocolatey fingers.

Chocolate-filled eggs are quite a surprise when you sit down to breakfast expecting to eat the hard-boiled variety.

THE BLOWN AND WAX-DIPPED EGGS

The art of blowing an egg is one of gentleness. First take your egg (whether it be hen, duck, goose or quail), wash it and gently ease a thick needle or hat pin through its top and then its base. At the base, peel a little of the shell away. Then, positioning the egg over a bowl, seal your lips over the egg top and blow forcefully. Like a balloon, the egg will at first be reluctant to come out and then it will suddenly squeeze out in a rush — it is not very pretty! Rinse the eggshell thoroughly and carefully in cold water and leave it propped up to dry. It is then ready to use.

Dipping eggs in wax and then food colouring is an excellent way of decorating eggs. The parts of the egg covered in wax resist the food dye and so stay as their original colour. Do be careful of the melted wax, however — it is probably best to wear rubber gloves to avoid accidentally burning yourself. My daughters were really most adventurous with their dying. They successfully combined colours to form all sorts of different shades.

WHAT YOU WILL NEED

Candle stubs

Saucepan

Food dyes (yellow, pink, blue)

Rubber gloves

Fine paintbrush (optional)

1 Melt the candle stubs gently in a saucepan.

2 Add a few drops of each food dye to tumblers of water.

3 Dip an egg into one colour of food dye, shake off the excess, and then dip it into the melted wax, just covering the dye mark. Then dip the egg back into the dye of your choice, and continue until you have achieved the result you require.

4 Alternatively, paint wax patterns over the egg before dipping it into a food dye.

THE PAPIER MACHE BOWLS

The added dimension to these little bowls are the rims. Follow the instructions on page 10 for the basic method of making papier mâché bowls. When they are dry, turn them upside down onto cardboard and mark a line around the bowl. Cut out the centre of the cardboard and discard it and then mark whatever shape of rim you wish to have on your bowls. Carefully cut out and attach each rim to its bowl with more strips of paper both on the top and underneath. Finish off like the main bowl.

For these papier mâché bowls I have used a scalloped edge decorated with blue spots, gentle curves decorated with blue spirals, and a round edge picking out the patterns from the quilt.

THE PATCHWORK TUMBLING BLOCK TABLECLOTH

Before beginning to sew, iron all your fabrics and trace and cut out the templates given below. Use these templates as your main set and cut out plenty more sets from scrap paper, and then cut out the fabric adding 6mm (¼in) seam allowances all the way around. To give the patchwork a three-dimensional effect, the top of each cube must be the lightest colour, the left side the darkest colour, and the right side the mid-colour. Although the shape of each piece is the same I have added stripes to show the directions they should fall to further the three-dimensional effect.

This tablecloth is made up of several hundred cubes, each of which is made from three pieces, so you will need to cut out plenty of templates and pieces of fabric. Have patience; this patchwork tablecloth took me one whole summer to stitch. I filled all the lost moments — travelling, watching television, listening to music, sitting in the sun — wherever I was, the patchwork was not far away.

WHAT YOU WILL NEED

Assorted fabrics

Scrap paper

Cotton thread

Needle

1 Fold each piece of fabric over a template and baste it in place — the templates can only be removed once each piece has been completely surrounded by other pieces of patchwork.

2 With right sides facing, hand stitch the covered templates together into cubes, one light, one dark and one mid-tone. Then sew each cube together to form your patchwork.

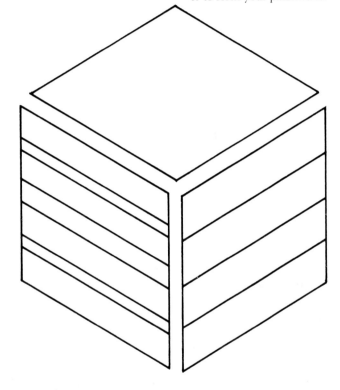

29

THE CHOCOLATE-FILLED EGGS

To melt chocolate successfully, the trick is to heat it on a very low heat over a saucepan one-quarter filled with simmering water.

WHAT YOU WILL NEED

100g (4oz) chocolate per egg

Blown eggs

Piping bag or teaspoon

1 Cut up two thirds of your chocolate quite finely and put it in a pudding bowl standing over the pan of simmering water. As the chocolate begins to melt, remove the bowl from the heat and add the remaining chocolate.

2 If you are filling a lot of eggs, put the melted chocolate into a piping bag and pipe the chocolate into the base of the hollow egg shells. Wipe away any spills as you go.

3 If you are filling only one or two eggs, dribble the chocolate into the hole in the base using a teaspoon.

4 Let the eggs harden naturally and then if you need to keep them for a few days, do so in the refrigerator. Don't leave them too long, however (as if that were possible), as heated chocolate is best eaten quickly.

Crack open the hard-boiled egg on Easter Sunday — and what a surprise, it's filled with chocolate.

BARBECUES

To eat and drink in the open air and cook as the light goes down is a very pleasurable experience.
I find preparing an abundance of sweetcorn and vegetables on kebabs irresistible. I love making everything
in advance and then leaving the men folk to become the cooks.

Barbecues are ideal for the very young with all the crumbs and discarded sausages tucked into the flowerbeds. They also are just the solution for the truculent adolescent who knows everything, from how to treat your best china to the raw essentials of cooking. So abandon yourself to simple crockery, mix and match glasses and let those who feel they know better eat the burnt offerings, while you enjoy your succulent morsel cooked over the glowing embers.

Barbecues are ideal if you are inviting guests with very diverse tastes as most foods can be arranged on metal skewers. Vegetables, as here, fish kebabs or a mixture of meats are all equally easy to thread onto the skewers. Everyone can select their meal according to their taste so have everything ready chopped and in bowls ready to be threaded at will. Some foods might need basting with olive oil, so have a small bowl of this to hand too. Some

foods are even easier to barbecue Sweetcorn cooks within its leaves, as do bananas over the embers. Wait until the skin turns a sweaty black and then peel it back and enjoy the most intense aroma and taste.

When stoking the barbecue choose the fuel that is local to your region, and never cook over open flames. Instead, wait until your fuel is white hot for the likes of sausages, or at a medium heat for more delicate foods. Denser foods require longer cooking so arrange foods on the grill and fan them out according to their needs. Small mushrooms and mussels will cook the moment they touch the grill, so cook them on the rim to offer as appetizers. Keep a water spray handy in case flames should suddenly flare up; this will prevent unnecessary burning.

Finally, one small suggestion — small goats' cheeses popped on a piece of bread lightly warmed above the embers are perfection with a glass of wine as your guests depart.

THE TOPIARY TOMATO TREE

The small tomato topiary tree featured in the photograph opposite is simple to make and easy to eat from, too. It can be re-used on numerous occasions during the year; sweet for birthday, or savoury for Christmas. It is a small indulgence, however, as it uses great quantities of tomatoes (or whatever you are covering it with — spinach, radishes, basil), but what a serving dish! Many times I have popped cheese and onions, dates and ham, pineapple and goats' cheese with a sprig of dill onto a tree like this. There are so many combinations; just stick them together with a cocktail stick and put into the tree.

At this barbecue, the tree rises above the table, does not take up too much room and looks spectacular. The full making instructions are on page 13, and it can be made up in any form, whether a cone, oval or round. Do have a go, it's very amusing to make.

Tomatoes galore on the topiary tree, and vegetable skewers and fresh sweetcorn roasting quietly; the aromas from this barbecue must be quite lovely.

THE LIGHTING

In the evening I enjoy lighting candles as they immediately create a warm ambience. Candles in metal cradles, like those in the photograph opposite, are ideal if little people are about. If the barbecue is for adults only, a festive way of using many candles is to place them in pretty jars suspended with wire in the branches of trees. Equally delightful are floating candles in bowls of water, a pond, or swimming pool (with the filter system turned off). To be practical, don't forget to buy a few candles infused with citronelle to deter insects.

Basil and spinach leaves wrapped around the tomatoes before they are stuck into the topiary tree add subtle flavours.

CHRISTENINGS

For some families, Christenings are the moment for everyone to gather together, sometimes even the whole village. It is wonderful to regroup after the service at your home with the small children of your contemporaries rushing around and the godparents, grandparents and maybe even great grandparents spoiling the baby of the day. Entertaining such numbers need not be difficult - prepare tiny cakes and bite-sized morsels and simply serve with tea, as I have done here.

A simply-set table is the best for such an occasion. With small things to eat there is no need to worry about cutlery - except, of course, the teaspoons for the tea - and it would be best if the china remained small and dainty for ease of carrying around and balancing on laps.

For this Christening I chose a floral theme and set about hand-embroidering the tablecloth with small cross-stitched rose buds. The china, too, picks up on this theme and the whole table is finished off with a charming small flower arrangement that features sweet-smelling spring flowers.

In Britain, it is traditional to keep the top layer of the wedding cake for the Christening. Before those who are not acquainted with British cakes are too shocked, the cake is thick with dried fruits with the minimum of mixture to hold it together. It is frequently cooked for several hours and laced with whisky. The marzipan and special icing sugar can preserve the cake for many years. After everyone has had their fill, cut up the cake into small pieces and hand these around. You might also like to keep some pieces to send to those guests and family who couldn't make the Christening.

Another tradition at Christenings is for each guest to give the baby a present. Usually this is something silver and personal such as a mug, napkin ring, jewellery or even a small set of cutlery; the baby's initials or name is frequently engraved on the item. It is lovely to be able to display the presents and if there is no room left on the tea table, the next best place would be a mantelpiece above a fireplace, just as I have done here. By propping the gifts up in their boxes and leaving the wrapping paper nestling among the presents, you can make a most attractive display.

The crisp white tablecloth embroidered with small roses sets off this Christening tea with great charm.

THE ROSE BUD TABLECLOTH

Each rose bud has been worked in cross stitch following the two charts opposite. The design works out quite delightfully and each bud is completed very quickly. Each rose bud is positioned at a random angle with the stems trailing up, down, and to the side, just as they do in nature. There are so many ways of using these little rose buds; extend the stems, join them together, or reverse them. Do experiment; it's fun. I hope that you will enjoy completing this cloth - if you wanted to, you could add more buds as the years go by.

WHAT YOU WILL NEED

Fabric (28 count chequered even-weave)

Pins

Embroidery threads:
shades of pink (DMC 899, 776)
shades of green (DMC 987, 3345, 890)

1 Mark the position of each rose on the fabric using pins to mark the centre point.

2 Following the charts opposite, work each rose bud. I have given two different designs of bud here and I found that the best way to work the tablecloth was to decide which bud I would stitch next as I got there.

3 Each square represents one cross. To give an even finish, make sure each stitch flows in the same direction.

BUNDLES OF SUGARED ALMONDS

One charming custom derived from the Latin countries of Europe is that of making up small bundles of sugared almonds to take home after the Christening. The almond is the symbol of purity, divine and natural innocence. This is why they are offered to those who attend a Christening tied up into small bundles. There are many beautiful ways of presenting them, but cutting tulle into circles the size of a dessert plate, adding ten white and ten blue or pink sugared almonds and then tying them with a tiny white bow is the most attractive, I think.

Bundles of pink and white sugared almonds and pink rose buds make very pretty additions to this baby girl's Christening.

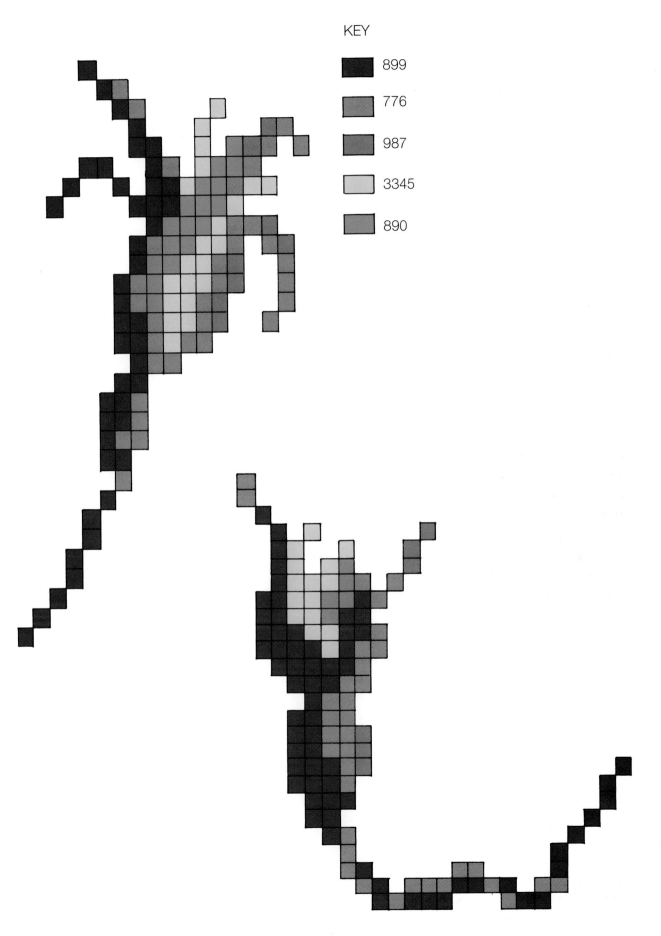

KEY

899

776

987

3345

890

CHILDREN'S PARTIES

My children's tastes at parties have never changed: pizza, sausages, crisps and cakes, followed by strawberries and ice cream for the more discerning. Don't make your life too complicated making tiny sandwiches that will only be ignored, instead have fun making a stencilled tablecloth out of a single sheet that can be used year after year. Or how about a gingerbread farmhouse accompanied by gingerbread animal biscuits?

Stencils are charming and practical for a simple cloth as they use very little fabric paint and yet exciting and colourful effects can be readily achieved. I have always prepared the table with the children but the smaller they were, the further away they were kept from the paint pot when stencilling. Load their brushes with paint and depending on their skill, they can decorate the cloth or paper napkins to match. Instructions for making these animal stencils are given overleaf and as well as being used for stencilling, the outlines can be used to make biscuits too (see overleaf again).

I like the theme of farm animals for small children as they lead to all sorts of games such as the farmer collecting the animals by sound; or biscuits strung across the room first as decoration and then as animals waiting to be leapt at to have a bite taken out of them. Hiding animal biscuits at the end of the party so that each child can collect their own farm is a great way to finish off the event — and avoids the expense of the party bag.

A gingerbread house is tasty, inexpensive, and the children will not have seen it before at the party last week. I have been looking back over my photographs and I came across a gingerbread castle that I made for my son's eighth birthday, complete with plastic knights that were a part of his birthday present. The castle was decorated with spy holes made from sweets — there was a particularly generous quantity on one side where my then six- and four-year-old daughters must have been 'helping'. Have a family go at all these ideas, they are fun and simple.

THE PULL-OUTS

Animal stencils on pages 47 and 49

See page 7 for how to use the pull- out section

Gingerbread animal biscuits decorated with trailing icing sugar are popping out from around the cups, waiting to see who will be sitting by them.

THE FARMYARD TABLECLOTH AND NAPKINS

I used a single sheet and spread it out on my table to see the positioning of the main design on the table. As the children sit at the table, a selection of animals face them and then more animals follow the plates around the table. However, feel free to scatter them wherever you like, or perhaps you might decide to make an animal border and paint other shapes in the middle. The paper napkins are a must at any children's party and look really good when stencilled to match the tablecloth.

WHAT YOU WILL NEED

Animal stencils (pages 47 and 49)

Cutting mat and knife

Masking tape

Fabric paints

Stencil brushes

1 Remove the tracing paper pull-outs from pages 47 and 49 and make them into stencils as outlined on page 9.

2 Position the stencils in your chosen places and keep in place with masking tape. Follow the instructions on page 9 for transferring the paint to the cloth.

3 I interspersed triangles, squares and circles as a loose border around the animals, choosing bright colours to reflect my plates and cups.

4 Repeat on the napkins.

The animal templates given on pages 47 and 49 are very versatile, making excellent decorations for the tablecloth and napkins, and outlines for delicious gingerbread biscuits.

THE GINGERBREAD ANIMAL BISCUITS

Prepare the animal stencils as described above, transfer the outlines (there is no need to transfer the stencil bridges) onto thin cardboard to make stronger templates and then cut them out. You will also need to adapt some of the outlines slightly — the pig's curly tail will have to be much smaller and the cock's tail less feathery. Children often love to decorate the animals, and you could add colours to the icing sugar for more lively animals. If your child doesn't like ginger, use cinnamon or ground almonds, or a little almond or vanilla essence works well too.

WHAT YOU WILL NEED

1 tsp bicarbonate of soda

2 tsp ground ginger

100g/4oz/$\frac{1}{2}$ cup butter

400g/14oz/3 cups plain (all-purpose) flour

175g/6oz/$\frac{3}{4}$ cups soft brown sugar

1 egg, beaten

60ml/4 tbsp golden syrup (corn syrup)

icing (confectioner's) sugar to decorate

food colourings (optional)

Makes 24 biscuits

1 Set the oven to 190°C/375°F/Gas Mark 5 and grease a baking sheet.

2 Put the bicarbonate of soda, ginger and butter in a bowl. Rub in the flour until it reaches a breadcrumb consistency. Then mix in the sugar and beaten egg.

3 Warm the syrup slightly to make it runny and stir it into the bowl to form a soft dough.

4 Lightly dust your worksurface with flour and then roll out part of the mixture. Cut around the animal templates, put on the baking sheet and leave to bake for 10 to 12 minutes. They become crisp on cooling.

5 Decorate the animals with icing sugar mixed with water and piped through a nozzle.

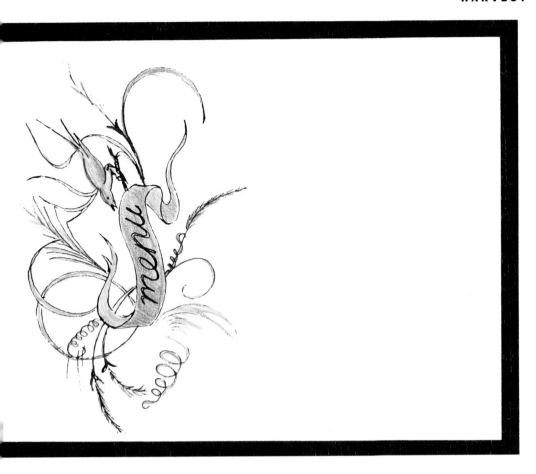

STAR STENCIL

(see page 16)

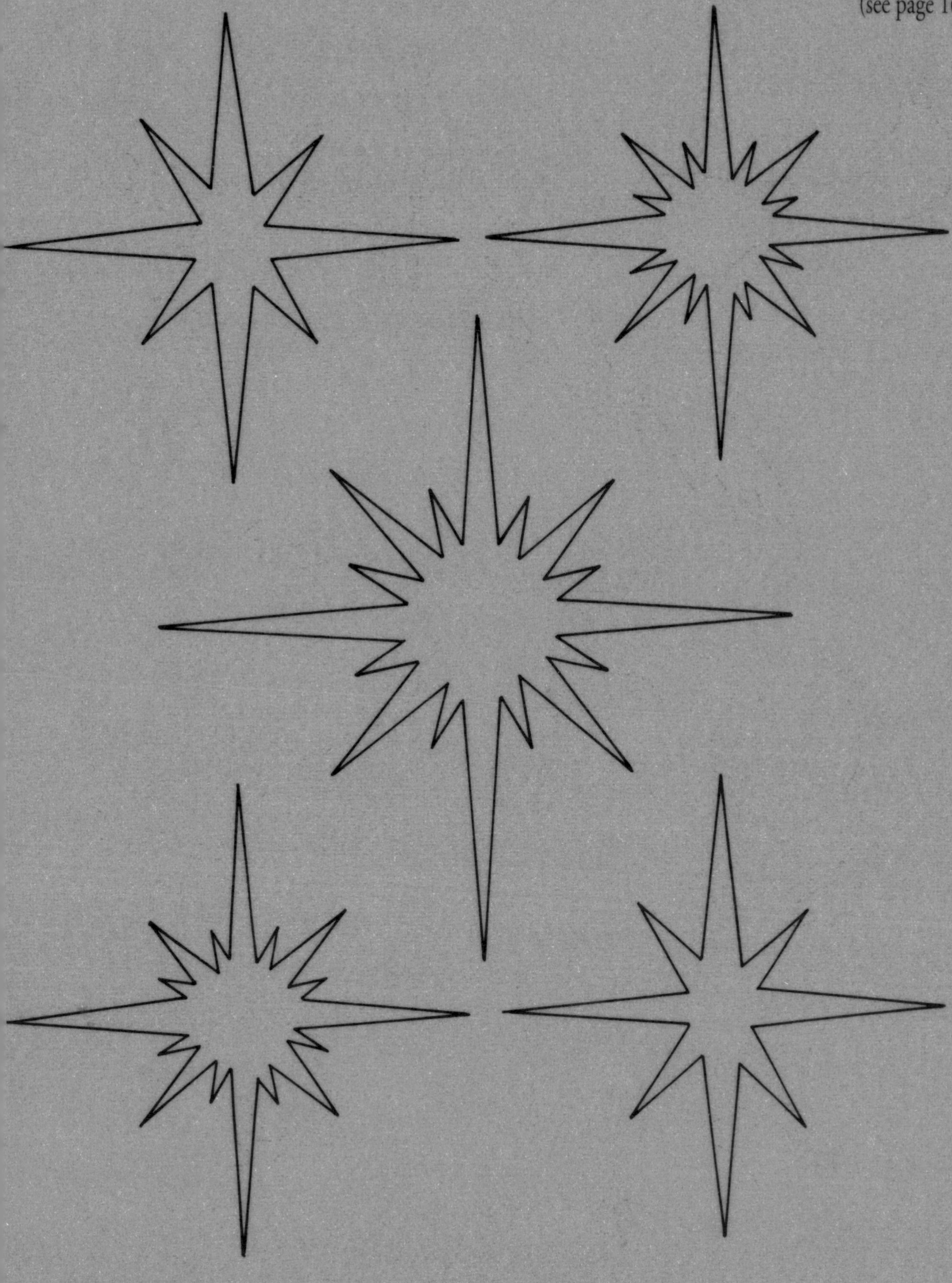

ANIMAL STENCILS
(see page 40)

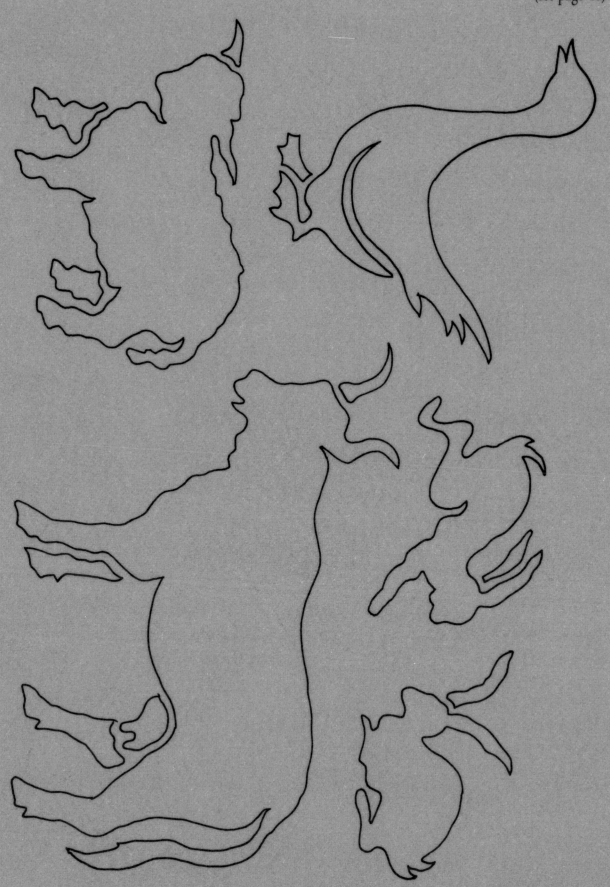

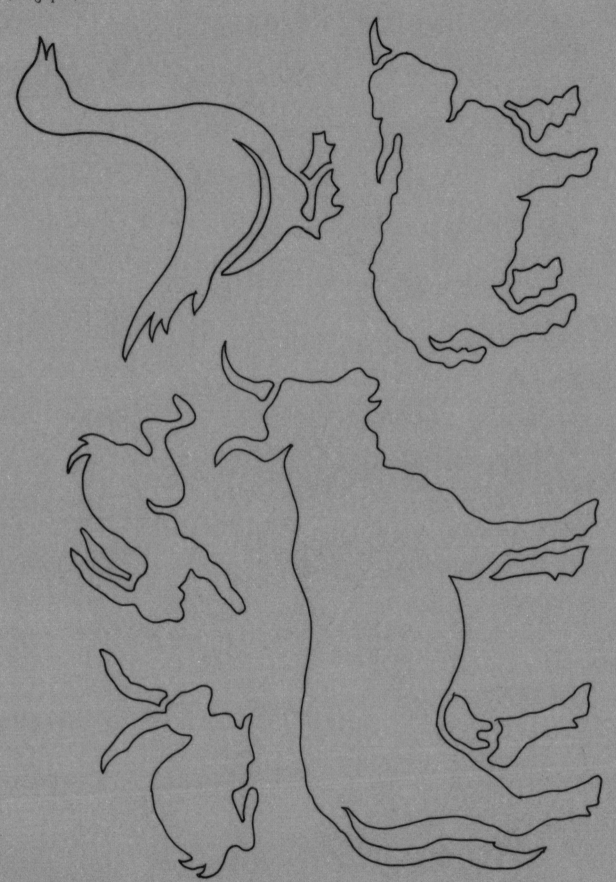

CHILDREN'S PARTIES
ANIMAL STENCILS
(see page 40)

VEGETABLE ETCHINGS
(see page 73)

THE GINGERBREAD HOUSE

To make a farmhouse like the one featured here you will need to double the ingredients given for the biscuits on page 40.

WHAT YOU WILL NEED

Scrap paper

Gingerbread biscuit ingredients, as on page 40

1 Make the templates for the house from the scrap paper. The roof template measures 31x15cm (12x6in); the front and back template measures 26x10cm (10x4in); and the side measures 19cm (7½in) wide and 10cm (4in) high rising to a central point, 19cm (7½in) from the base line.

2 Set the oven to 190°C/375°F/Gas Mark 5 and grease a baking sheet.

3 Make the gingerbread mixture, as on page 40, but when you have rolled out the mixture gently roll it onto your rolling pin and transfer it onto the baking tray. Then, and only then, cut out the house using the templates. Cut two of each template. If you transfer the mixture once it is cut it will distort slightly, and you will end up with a wobbly house that is very difficult to put together. Remember to cut out any windows and doors that you want to appear in the finished house.

4 Bake the mixture until brown as you want it to be a little stronger than the biscuits. Leave to cool on the baking tray.

5 On the board or tray on which you will be making the house (gingerbread houses don't like being moved), start by gluing the sides of the house together. Use icing sugar mixed with water as glue and tins or jars to prop the walls upright. Leave the supports in place until the icing sugar has dried and then attach the roof in the same way.

6 Decorate the house with drizzles of icing sugar mixed with water, and add food coloured details.

The roof of this house has been decorated with a fine trellis to imitate roof tiles, and there are plenty of plants growing up its sides from colourful pots.

WEDDINGS

Weddings are a time of hope, happiness, and kisses. The joining together of families to create another is most definitely worthy of celebration. It is the most memorable of days, full of atmosphere. So amaze your guests, tuck fabulous flowers into unexpected places for them, and make sure there is a never ending supply of overflowing glasses.

The wedding table is best simply laid and beautifully decorated to receive and welcome your guests. Intertwine the bride and groom's initials, a true symbol of unity, and softly mark them out in gold over a muslin tablecloth. To further the theme, trace the same design — this time reduced — onto place and menu cards, and also embroider the napkins with the initials.

The guests will spend more time being received at the wedding table than they do at the service. It will also be the first opportunity for introducing themselves to each other so make sure there is plenty to occupy them in terms of food and drink. The intertwining initials will certainly invite comments and cause amusement. The place cards enable the guests to promenade the table, chatting here and there while enjoying the scene, and the menu cards reveal the feast to come.

Floral arrangements in soft greens and whites with blushing roses are subtle and beautiful for a wedding table. My favourite flowers are white and those that have a heady perfume. The arrangements featured in these photographs were created by my mother, with me as assistant. Such comments as, "hold the tape, don't do this, don't do that" were all too frequently being hurled in my direction. I decided that tall, flowing arrangements that were not too dense would be ideal because then the guests seated across the table could still talk through the stems.

For each arrangement, the flowers are firmly fixed into a piece of florist's foam. This has been cut to the shape of the vase top and taped firmly in place with non-porous tape over plastic wrap loosely suspended in the flute vase. My mother first arranged the main foliage structure, in this case eucalyptus. Then she added more green foliage in various shades of light green and finally the smaller white narcissus and roses. Last came the white lilies which were carefully positioned as they are the focal points of the arrangements. Full instructions for the little candle arrangement featured opposite are given on page 12.

Opposite: *Narcissus, freesias and creamy roses are all incredibly fragrant flowers; and lit by candlelight, the final effect is softly caressing.*

Overleaf: *The wedding table laid ready for the arrival of the bride and groom and their guests. Notice how the happy couple's entwined letters flow over the edges of the tablecloth.*

THE CALLIGRAPHY TABLECLOTH, PLACE CARDS AND MENUS

Using my initials and those of my partner, I combined A St G with A G M, which gave me A St G M. When creating the design, I was inspired by the wonderful calligraphy on the plates and decided to emulate the lettering. However, there are many calligraphy books available if you want to try another style.

I drew each letter separately on tracing paper and then played with them, superimposing one over the other, moving the letters in and out until I was happy with the inter-link-ing that was made. I then traced the interlinked initials onto paper and enlarged and reduced them on a photocopier to have a choice of sizes.

For the tablecloth, place the initialized paper beneath some muslin cut to the size of table you wish to cover. Then simply trace through the initials onto the cloth using a gold felt-tipped pen. Use muslin, organza, cheesecloth, or even light silk — any fabric that is light enough to see the initials through. I used gold, which washes out, but indeli-ble felt-tipped pens don't wash out.

The place cards and menus are cut out of smooth watercolour paper and folded to make them stand. I didn't feel that the chances of being able to achieve perfect calligraphy on each card were good, so I traced our initials faintly onto each card and then went over the tracing with a fine gold felt-tipped pen. Once the ink had dried, I rubbed out any pencil marking that might show. Cards could also be made to thank the guests for their gifts or add the initials to your invitations.

Above: *The entwined initials on the tablecloth, place card and menu really help to unite a table setting.*

Opposite: *This place setting is simple and yet so refined. The gold and silver, blue and white, look quite lovely together.*

THE
EMBROIDERED NAPKIN

Satin stitched initials embroidered onto linen are a rewarding gift to offer the wedding guests to remind them of the happy day. I chose blue to contrast with the antique white linen, and to tone with the blues in the plates. Alternatively, you could stitch white on white which is ravishing and yet discreet.

You could either stitch the outlines on a sewing machine, of the sophisticated variety, or by hand, although this is most definitely time consuming. Trace the initials onto your linen (see the letter A given left), and stitch the outline in satin stitch using washable stranded cotton in the colour of your choice.

PICNICS

I have finally learnt that a truly pleasurable picnic is one that is impromptu, grabbing the odd hour of sun or an unexpected free moment. Whatever your expedition, whether you are sailing, sitting on the beach, out walking in woods, country or on mountains, or cycling to discover the unknown or in the nearby park — take a picnic. Don't bother with endless plastic boxes, eat the food out of its natural packaging, just as I have done here. It is much more fun, makes for much less waste, and there is no chasing after plastic bags in the wind.

For my picnic in its natural packaging, I have chosen to use de-seeded green peppers filled with salad and cheese, a large Savoy cabbage hollowed out to use as a salad bowl with a chopped mixed salad nestling in its leaves, and sandwiches re-stacked back in the centre of the loaf of bread. It's a perfect container, just made for the job. Each of these foods is described overleaf.

If you should be after something a little sweeter to follow on from the sandwiches and salads, how about a scooped out melon filled with strawberries, melon balls, blanched almonds, and sprigs of mint? Or a pineapple with its centre removed like the loaf of bread, cut into slices and replaced with a squeeze of lemon between the layers? A fresh

coconut cut in half and filled with fresh dates and baby goats' cheeses is equally wonderful.

I have also chosen large shells for my plates as they are light and were they to chip, it would only be nature's wear. Frequently, you need a good knife on a picnic for shellfish, fruit and cheese, and these folding knives and forks are just the thing to have. Designed for cheese tasting, they are good to hold and don't break. I also really like to have a glass to drink out of and the stacking variety, such as those featured opposite, are ideal for a picnic. Put everything into a wooden picnic basket and you can carry it with ease, or attach it to the back of a bicycle just as I do: this basket has travelled far with me and remains a good friend.

In addition to the wonderfully tasty food, all in its natural packaging, all you need to take for a most relaxing picnic is a rug to sit on and perhaps some cushions on which to rest your head.

THE FOOD IN ITS NATURAL PACKAGING

Much seafood comes in its own packaging, so the shells left behind on a beach would not worry me, but plastic boxes and yogurt cartons are better left at home. All the ideas included in this picnic are very straightforward to make, and here are the details.

1 To use a Savoy cabbage or iceberg lettuce, slice a quarter off the top. Then cut out the inside and mix with other ingredients of your choice. I love cabbage with apple, walnuts, and small gratings of fresh ginger all mixed in a natural yogurt and orange juice dressing followed by a coarse grating of black pepper.

2 Red and green peppers are natural individual containers for delicious morsels. I like cheese and vegetables in green peppers, and charcuterie and salad in red peppers. Rice and tuna with nutmeg and pine nuts is good and spoons well into a pepper, while more delicate flavours of prawns and salad complement the more subtle yellow and orange peppers. Pop the pepper tops back on and tie them up in a napkin ready for eating.

3 For sandwiches, cut the top off the loaf with a very sharp knife. Then cut gently down the sides taking care that you don't cut too far, chopping the bottom off accidentally. Slide the knife into the loaf just above the base and ease it across one half of the loaf base trying not to cut the crust any more than you have to. Pull the knife out, turn it over and cut the other half of the base. Gently ease the bread out of its crust. Make up your sandwiches, and then replace the bread slices in the same order as they were removed. Put the lid back on and wrap up the loaf to keep it intact — I use cotton headscarves. (You can also remove the centres of little buns in the same way. They make charming containers that are good for all sorts of goodies, whether they be savoury, vegetable or very spicy.)

Right: *A glass of wine is the perfect accompaniment for these naturally packed foods.*

Below: *After a picnic like this all you need to take home are the plates, cutlery and picnic rug.*

BUSINESS
BREAKFASTS

When travelling for business, breakfast can be a good time to catch people, particularly with time differences between countries; it could be your associates' liveliest time. With a pot of piping hot coffee and juice and toast to hand, any meeting will start well.

Avery large napkin is essential, to protect your business clothes for the coming day's meetings, and trays are easy as they can be placed anywhere depending on how much work needs to be spread out. The embroidered napkins set out on this breakfast tray are embroidered with elements from the business pages of the daily newspapers, which I think add a touch of humour to such important business meetings.

THE EMBROIDERED NAPKINS

Each napkin has a different design, both taken from newspapers.
To create your own napkins follow the lettering below. The wavy lines are made by free stitching on the Dossier napkin.

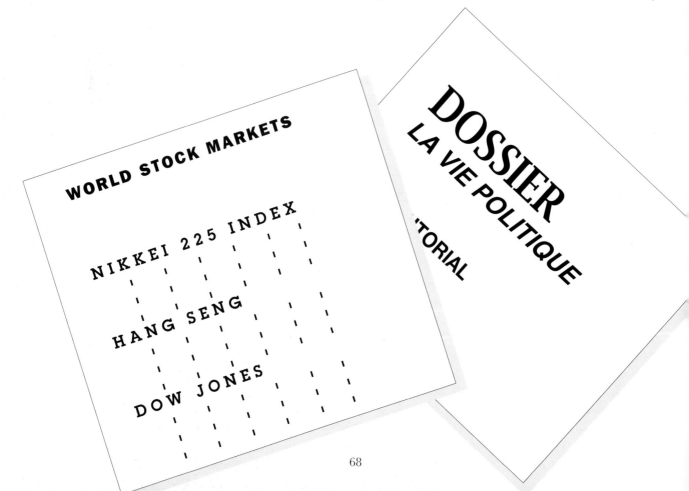

1 Spread out some daily newspapers and trace off various bits of text that catch your eye on the business pages. Copy exactly the same typeface of the newspaper and even the same size of type (alternatively, you could enlarge or reduce type on a photocopier to suit your needs).

2 Trace the words onto the right side of the napkin and on the wrong side iron on some interfacing to stiffen the fabric. Then either embroider using a sewing machine or hand stitch using satin stitch. On finer linens try to avoid trailing threads between letters on the back as they will show through on the front.

3 If you are hand stitching, use only two strands of the cotton to prevent the back of the napkin from becoming too bulky.

4 When the stitching is completed, gently peel away the interfacing on the back, clipping neatly with embroidery scissors where it is held by the stitching. Wash as normal for linen.

Chrome, black and white is a very elegant combination of colours, ideal for a smart business breakfast meeting.

DINING
AL FRESCO

Eating al fresco is usually an impromptu affair, grabbing the sun while it lasts. Here is a découpaged table that gathers the full harvest of vegetables, swirling them around in a continual cycle of fresh abundance. When eating in a relaxed way, perhaps using up what is in the fridge and sharing it with a friend, it is charming to already have coordinating items for your table. On these pages, I show you exactly how to do this, starting with those fresh, but découpaged, vegetables.

I love to etch, so I bought this inexpensive green metal table and set about decorating it with my etchings of vegetables. After drawing a wide selection — here you can see radishes, corn on the cob, onions, cabbages and garlic — I photocopied the vegetables and coloured them in with colouring pencils. After gluing them to the table top the last stage was to protect them with many layers of varnish. Detailed instructions for découpage are given on page 11 and some of the coloured images are provided in the pull-out section on page 54. Other ways to decorate an outside table could be with flower images from magazines or seed packets, or how about making your own sketches? This form of decorating really is most rewarding.

I also used some of the radish etchings on the papier mâché bowls that look so colourful and decorative in the centre of the table. Coordinating a table when decorating it is an entertaining challenge. As well as using découpaged radishes on the bowls, I also decided to stitch them onto the napkins using satin stitch (see overleaf for detailed instructions). Why not trace an image from your crockery and transfer it onto a napkin or tablecloth in the same way?

Each of these ideas is inexpensive to recreate and the end result is unique. The table immediately looks dressed, even if you are still chopping up the vegetables for your meal or piling up the plates and cutlery before eating.

THE PULL-OUTS

Vegetable etchings on page 54

See page 7 for how to use the pull-out section.

The art of découpage is straightforward and here the end result is informal, designed to make the table look dressed at all times.

THE RADISH NAPKIN

This little radish is very simple to work using satin stitches. As the radish is round I have let my stitches flow in a curve giving the radish a natural shape. Straight stitches would give a flattened radish — not very appetizing.

1 Trace the image given on this page onto your linen. To do this, trace the outline onto tracing or parchment paper. Then go over the lines on the reverse side with a soft pencil and pin the tracing onto the napkin where you want the image to be stitched. Finally, draw over the lines one more time on the top side of the tracing or parchment paper and remove it before starting to stitch.

2 Stitch the darker tones of red on one side, building over the round radish into lighter, warmer reds. Add a dash of cream for the highlight. Make sure that the satin stitches fit snuggly into one another without gaps as these might make a radish look rather moth eaten.

3 On the leaves, use the central vein as a natural divider and satin stitch one side in one shade of green, and the other in the contrasting shade. Varying the tones of your stranded cotton gives additional movement to your work.

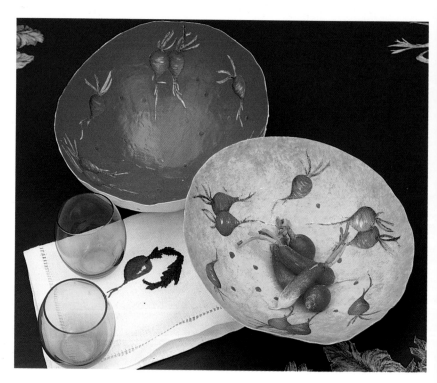

Two papier mâché bowls and a napkin, each featuring the radish design, show how easy it is to coordinate a table setting.

72

THE PAPIER MACHE BOWLS

The instructions for making papier mâché bowls are also fully explained on page 10. Have fun decorating your bowls, especially with your choice of colours. I decided to add a speckled tone to the yellow bowl to coordinate with the plates, and the vibrant red interior of the other bowl contrasts beautifully with the green table and yet still supports the red radish image. Finally, coordinate your work by using copies of the same motif (or two or three), that appears on the table, gluing them over the inside and outside edges of the bowl. See the découpage instructions on page 11 and add the coats of varnish after the images are stuck in place.

THE DECOUPAGED TABLE

The instructions for découpage are fully explained on page 11 and some of the etchings are provided on page 54. All the same rules apply for this table top. However, do be more thorough with your gluing and varnishing, especially if your table remains outside. First, use EVA glue (a waterproof version of PVA), and then protect your table with abundant layers of varnish — I used fifteen. Ask your local supplier to recommend the best brand of varnish, and stress that whatever you are varnishing remains outside. My table has survived the damp and continual drizzle of England, even an exceptionally blistering hot summer. However, during the winter I leave it tilted so that the water at least runs off it.

When colouring in etchings it is important to use many shades of the same colour to give the end result a fluid and natural feel.

HARVEST THANKSGIVING

During the autumn there is an abundance of overflowing fruits, nuts, flowers and vegetables.
It is a short season and yet the year's wealth is summed up in it. Even in the biggest city or most industrial
town, the trees spill shiny conkers, delicious beechnuts are trodden underfoot, and the spiky
sweet chestnut is rarely missed. So choose the finest wine and dress your table and room with fruits and
flowers, and savour the richness of the season.

When inviting friends for a feast, I like to prepare a meal that is easily passed around the table, with mixed vegetables following close behind. It is important for me to have time to catch up with conversation so I want the food to be rewarding but not an intrusion on my time at the table. In addition, I find that menu cards are an attractive decoration and they help to structure the evening, building anticipation for the delights to come. The menu cards on this table setting are featured on page 41 in the pull-out section. They appear as black and white cards in the photograph opposite, but I also enjoy making them more colourful, to fit in with the table's theme. The cards at the centre of the book have been coloured for just this reason. Cut them out as described on page 7.

I find that floral centrepieces softly lit with bees' wax candles are warm and welcoming. I chose fresh flowers, reflecting the golden shades of autumn and arranged them as a long and low centrepiece so that it wouldn't interrupt conversation across the table. I also used the same colours for the garland of dried flowers hanging from the fireplace. Fruits, leaves and flowers have been wired together to celebrate further the abundance of autumn. Detailed instructions are given overleaf for making both the arrangements and the garland.

To me, smell is the most potent sense, and I have set out to create a wonderfully aromatic table setting here. Flowers, bees' wax candles, the food, wine followed by Armagnac, and essential oils on the dried flowers (a little orange oil rubbed into the wrists is divinely relaxing) combine to create a deliciously perfumed evening.

THE PULL-OUTS

Menu cards on page 41

See page 7 for how to use the
pull-out section.

---

*The bright red napkins enhance the red flowers in the floral arrangements,
making this a truly autumnal table setting.*

THE FAN NAPKINS

Each napkin on this table has been folded in the shape of a fan adding a new dimension to the setting. The folded fan is easy to achieve (see page 91 for making instructions) and could even be folded while being ironed. Napkins folded in this way are very practical to store as closed fans.

THE FRESH FLOWER ARRANGEMENT

In this flower arrangement I used freesias, chrysanthemums, lilies, mimosas and chillies; the last adds a touch of humour to the arrangement as they are so unusual in this setting. However, any selection of flowers would do; use what you can lay your hands on, but remember to use colours that tone well together.

WHAT YOU WILL NEED

Florist's foam

Oval cooking dish

Florist's tape

Candles

Selection of cut flowers

Greenery

1 Cut the florist's foam to the right size for the cooking dish and fasten in place with florist's tape.

2 Position the candles in the centre of the dish, planting them in the florist's foam.

3 Arrange the flowers and greenery to reflect the oval shape of the cooking dish. Ensure that some ends of flowers and greenery touch the table, and even a plate or two, so that the arrangement appears less formal.

4 Water the arrangement thoroughly and keep topping it up frequently as all those flowers will be very thirsty.

Napkins folded as exotically as these ones are not very difficult to achieve, and the end result is well worth it (see page 91 for folding instructions).

THE DRIED FLOWER GARLAND

The easiest way to make a solid base for this garland is to wrap florist's foam in chicken wire. Pull and push the chicken wire until you have the shape you require and then secure it in place.

The many dried Chinese lanterns and gourds used in this flower garland bring shades of autumn into the home.

WHAT YOU WILL NEED

Florist's foam

Chicken wire

Dried flowers (such as Chinese lanterns, ivy, hydrangeas)

Dried fruits (such as gourds)

Florist's wire

1 First insert the lighter ingredients, such as the dried flowers, through the chicken wire and into the florist's foam.

2 Then fill up spaces with the heavier items. For gourds, wind a length of florist's wire around the ends, insert the wire through the chicken wire and wrap them together tightly.

3 Slowly build up the arrangement. I place the largest pieces in the centre and work out to the edges where the smaller ingredients are inserted. However, there are no rules. If you don't like what you have done, just pull out the offending pieces and have another go. Equally, if ingredients look tired after a while, replace them with other goodies as the months pass. Harvest flowers and fruits will soon be replaced by oddments sprayed gold for Christmas.

FORMAL
CELEBRATIONS

To host a formal evening can often be daunting as you might feel that you need to create a smart look within your home. I felt just like this one day so decided to set about découpaging a set of etchings on the wall of my dining room. I then took it one step further by découpaging a set of table mats, napkin rings and I even made some table lampshades to match, too.

The one advantage to formal evenings is that you have plenty of notice since invitations are sent out and replies received weeks in advance, so you will have lots of time to think about your table setting. Start at the beginning of your setting and work up to the decorative details. So, why not use a thick material, like this white quilted bedspread, for your tablecloth? It will certainly be cause for comments and will be a rich setting on which to place your china and cutlery. Lighting, too, is important and must be good. I find that candle lamps such as those used in the photograph opposite combine elegance with a marvellous atmosphere.

For the découpaged wall I first drew a series of pictures based on a floral theme and then linked them with a series of swags, frames and other decorative devices. Of course, it took a great deal of measuring and marking on the wall to check that everything was centred and straight, but I think that the end result is definitely worth it.

Detailed instructions for découpage are given on page 11. For the mats and napkin rings I used details taken from the picture frames (for making instructions, see overleaf). With forethought, these decorative details are easily achieved and give the dining table setting a sophisticated chic.

THE PULL-OUTS

Lampshade on page 56

See page 7 for how to use the pull-out section.

Uniquely decorated table mats and napkin rings add detailed interest to the restrained dining table.

THE LAMPSHADES

One of these lampshades is given on page 56 in the pull-out section. After cutting it out as described on page 7, spread some all-purpose glue along the overlap edge indicated by the dotted line. Join the two edges together and hold in place with paper-clips until the glue is dry. Then attach to a candle follower. Always use a straight-sided candle in one of these and don't leave it unsupervised.

  If you should decide to use the lampshade with a light bulb rather than a candle, make sure that the bulb isn't too close to the paper shade. There should be a minimum clearance of 3cm (1¼in) between a 40 watt bulb and a shade such as this one. Furthermore, a 40 watt bulb is the maximum wattage that we recommend using with this paper shade. Bulb clips are ideal for using under lampshades and are readily available.

Small lampshades lit by candlelight are unobtrusive and the lighting is most atmospheric.

THE DECOUPAGE PLACE MATS AND NAPKIN RINGS

The full making instructions for découpage are given on page 11 but here are a few additional tips for the mats.

1 The circular design given opposite is suitable for round mats but the central sprig design could be used on round or rectangular mats.

2 If the designs do not fit your mats (or perhaps a tray that you wish to use for découpage), simply reduce or enlarge them on a photocopier to an appropriate size.

I reduced the piece of découpage on this table mat many times over on a photocopier to achieve a suitably small design for the napkin ring. The napkin edges have been made by stitching on lengths of gold ribbon using a sewing machine (see page 16 for making instructions).

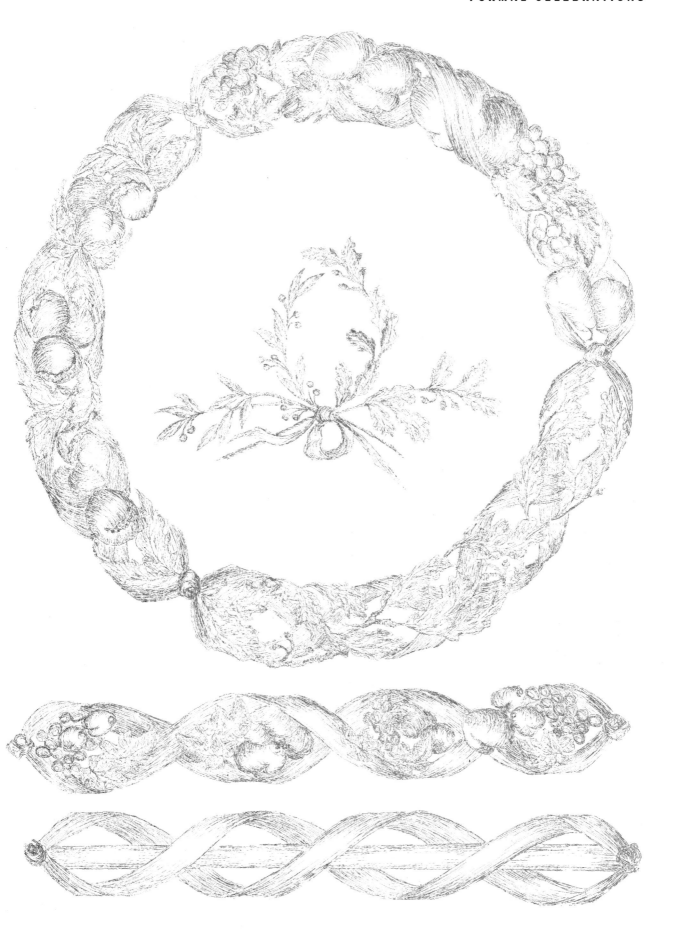

CHRISTMAS

Christmas is a wonderful time of the year. It is a time of giving to family and friends and celebrating religious beliefs and family reunions. There is lots of wrapping — and unwrapping — to do and now is the time to prepare new decorations and rediscover the old ones stored away from last year. To me, the most important elements of Christmas are the dining table and the Christmas tree.

I think that sitting at a beautifully decorated Christmas dining table for hours surrounded by friends and family is one of the greatest luxuries. Every family has their own rituals on Christmas day, particularly on opening presents, and I like to have a tiny something wrapped on each plate as I think this is most welcoming.

Stencilling is quick and easy and can be used on delicate tissue paper for wrapping, on card for labels and beneath glass plates. Stencil the tablecloth, napkins and place mats, and why not even stencil your kitchen apron to bring a touch of the festive to that all-too-frequently forgotten room? It is easy to coordinate your whole setting with this adaptable holly and mistletoe stencil. It is featured on page 51 in the pull-out section, and detailed instructions for using the stencil are given on pages 8-9.

For the Christmas table setting featured opposite and overleaf, a French family was invited so I turned the fork into the table which is correct in France; each country has its own etiquette. The champagne flute is filled awaiting the arrival of the guests, and there are red and white wine glasses poised, ready to be filled at later stages during the meal.

Atmospheric lighting is all-important at Christmas and it is easily achieved with candles. Here simple night lights that are easily replaceable cast a flickering warmth over the table. On the mantelpiece they softly illuminate the crib scene, and, of course, miniature candles are lighting the tree. A candle-lit tree is an exquisite treat. These candles (it is best to find safety ones) have been attached to the tree using simple clip-on candle holders made from tin.

THE PULL-OUTS

Holly and mistletoe stencil on page 51

Star stencil on page 45

See page 7 for how to use the pull-out section.

Opposite: *Here the holly and mistletoe stencil can be seen on the glass plates, napkin, present labels and the wrapping paper. It is truly flexible unites the table in a festive way.*

Overleaf: *Presents are crammed onto the table and beneath the Christm tree. Each has been wrapped in stencilled tissue paper and tied with brig coloured ribbons. The choice of colours for the paper has been limited to g and blue to add to the sophisticated air of this table setting.*

THE STENCILLED PLATES

These glass plates are fun and to stencil them temporarily on the underside adds festivity to the Christmas feast. I stencilled beneath them both for hygienic purposes and to ensure that the stencil would survive all the knife scratchings a plate endures during a meal. To remove spray paints either use a dishwasher or if the plates won't tolerate a dishwasher, use nail varnish remover. Spray paint resists normal light washing.

WHAT YOU WILL NEED

Holly and mistletoe stencil (page 51)

Cutting mat and knife

Masking tape

Spray or glass paints (gold, reds, greens)

Paintbrush (for glass paints only)

1 Remove the tracing paper pull-out from page 51 and make it into a stencil as outlined on page 9.

2 Select the part of the design you wish to use and stick down the stencil with masking tape. Make sure it is particularly well stuck down over any curves and ridges.

3 Spray on the paints or paint them on, depending on your choice of paints. Remove the stencil.

THE NAPKINS AND PLACE MATS

Stencilling with fabric paint using the stippling method is fully explained on page 9 and the smart way the napkins are folded is explained on page 92. To seal the fabric paints for washing, iron on the reverse side at the temperature the fabric can take.

These napkins are finished organza, but a pretty, fresh unfinished cotton could be fun just for a few days over Christmas. The beauty of stencilling is that it does not always have to be permanent.

I also stencilled some place mats to match the napkins as a variation to the table setting featured on the previous pages. I used the total design and it is rather nice to see it showing through the glass plates. The stencil on the plates means that the design will be seen in layers, creating a lovely, three-dimensional effect.

The table is laid, the wine is poured, the meal is about to begin. Here, the holly and mistletoe motif has been stencilled onto the napkin, plates and table mat creating a three-dimensional effect.

THE WRAPPED PRESENTS

It always amazes me how much paper is needed to wrap all those Christmas presents, and as I love to pile all my presents under the tree I used to be forever dashing out for another roll. That is until I discovered how inexpensive and straightforward it is to make wrapping paper. Take any paper, whether it be brown paper, rice paper, tissue paper, or anything else you like that folds — even muslin or cheesecloth will do — and decorate with all of or only part of a stencil design.

There are two stencil designs given in the middle of this book (see pages 45 and 51) that are suitable for Christmas. Prepare them as explained on pages 8-9 and then use spray paint — I used gold, reds and greens — to stencil on the designs. Spray paints are very quick to use but ensure that you are in a well-ventilated room. If children are using stencils, it is best that they use acrylic paints and stipple brushes (also see page 9 for information on stippling). They can make cards to send and labels to write on. For my labels, I cut around the leaf stencils to make a shaped card which I think is very pretty.

A pile of wrapped presents piled beneath the Christmas tree — what a festive sight.

87

ETIQUETTE

Both etiquette and manners are a set of rules for polite behaviour. My experience of understanding basic etiquette is that it puts everyone at ease so that they can enjoy themselves. Also, once you understand the rules, you can then adapt them to your requirements.

Having sent invitation cards stating the time, venue and dress, or telephoned your guests to invite them to dine, now is the time to prepare your menu together with your wines. This will then determine how you will lay the table. Throughout the year, festivities will influence the table setting. It is also well worth preparing a seating plan.

The menu will reflect the skills of the cook, the budget, and help available. It is important never to attempt too much, nor to cook something new. The greatest failure of any dinner party is the prolonged absence of the hostess or host. Attention to your guests must take precedence over the food planned. So try to keep food simple and fresh, it is the easiest and best. It should be a pleasure for you to receive your guests as a good welcome sets the atmosphere for the evening ahead. So be kind to yourself and prepare as much as possible in advance.

Correct Order of Laying the Table

GLASSES
These are placed over the knife, normally in a convenient order for drinking out of. The French place their glasses more centrally. Always include a water tumbler or large wine glass, and water should be available throughout the meal.

NAPKINS
These are either folded prettily (see pages 91-2) in the centre of the place setting or placed on the bread plate on the left in a rectangle. Napkin rings can be used for decoration, and are useful for identification.

Table linen is most appropriate for entertaining, and red wines are enhanced by a white, cream or pink cloth; white wines are complemented by most colours.

CANDLES
These are desirable for evening dining as they are most flattering and kind, adding warmth - even when light is not required. I adore candles as they create a marvellous atmosphere. Dip your lighting a little in order to appreciate them to their utmost. I find strong lighting most objectionable in the evening at table and have frequently asked restaurants to accommodate me accordingly. Sometimes lighting is so strong I wonder if I have left the office!

FLOWERS
Flowers are wonderful whether as a full arrangement or a flower tucked into a napkin. So always try to include them in your table settings. Also, think of the now readily available essential oils, or the old-fashioned lavender or rose waters. A touch on a napkin can be a delightful treat.

CONDIMENTS
Salt, pepper, and mustard should be laid on the table, if needed, but remove them before anything sweet arrives; and always remember to serve water throughout the meal.

Wines and Liqueurs

Always offer your guests an aperitif as they arrive and are introduced to one another. Aperitifs are usually served with small titbits, such as baby vegetables or small cânapés, or even nuts and other such nibbles. Champagne is universally acceptable. Some have touches of fruits, which are fun in the summer months. In Latin countries you will be offered port, mixed wine-derivative drinks, and long spirit drinks such as vodka tonic, gin and tonic, and wine. In the States I have been offered all sorts of things, and most of the names sound quite divine. However, I like to be simple and enjoy the meal, so I stay with Champagne or wine.

The temperature of wines is important. Red wines are normally served at room temperature and opened before the meal to breath. Older wines are served slightly tilted in baskets to avoid movement. Those wines with sediment should be decanted through a sieve; do this slowly and carefully and let the wine trickle into the decanter, disturbing it to the minimum.

Beaujolais is a light red wine and so it can be served chilled, particularly if you are drinking it the same year as it was bottled. Dry sherry, white wine and Champagne are also served chilled.

AFTER THE MEAL

Always serve coffee and a choice of liqueurs and spirits if available, together with cigarettes or cigars. Occasionally, women withdraw and the men remain at the table, joining the women later. Some of the older generation still apply this rule. However, the last time I was invited to withdraw, all of the men bar two followed the women, claiming their conversation to be more amusing.

GLASSES

The reason for so many and varied glasses are that for the true connoisseur it is the shape of the glass that controls the direction in which the wine flows onto the tongue. The glass becomes the match-maker between the characteristics of the wine and the way in which it is tasted. For example, white wine is served in a smaller glass than red, as often white wines are sweeter so the smaller glass allows you to sip at the wine. It is then directed to the tip of your tongue where the maximum sweet taste buds are situated. Most red wine glasses are larger as the wine is then directed to the centre of the tongue; and the wider bowl allows the wine to breath.

On being presented with wine it is appropriate to appreciate the wine's bouquet before drinking. Wine should always be sipped and the glass put back in place between each sip. On finishing a good wine with friends at the end of a meal, you might choose to cradle the wine glass and enjoy the bouquet to the full; take the cue from your hostess.

Glasses should be changed or washed at each change of wine. It is perfectly correct to refuse wine at any point during the meal; simply say, 'no thank you'.

FOOD AND WHAT TO DRINK WITH IT

Soup
Sherry

Shellfish and fish
Dry white wine

Highly-seasoned red meat and game
Full-bodied, heavy red wine, typically a Burgundy

Other red meats
Lighter red wines, such as a Bordeaux

White meats
Light red wines, medium-dry white, and rose

Cheese
Red wine or port

Desserts
Sweet white wines or Champagne

The Guest

International manners are difficult to define as what is acceptable in one country may not be in another. However, as I am always instilling in my children, you are judged on your behaviour, particularly at table. Certain rules, although basic, are international. For example, flowers, chocolates or beautiful sweets are internationally acceptable as a present to your hostess. However, other rules vary from country to country. For example, you should turn up on time in Anglo Saxon countries, but be late in Latin ones. Likewise, in France and other Latin countries, small children are presented and very little ones might kiss you once on each cheek while slightly older ones might offer a hand to shake. In other European countries, even the smallest children offer a hand to shake. Sometimes, small token presents are given to the children, par-

ticularly if you have met them previously, and a few words are exchanged. The children will then retire to bed.

At table, always wait to be seated and men should wait a moment longer until the women are sitting. Be courteous to those on either side of you, both conversationally and checking to see if they require anything on the table, even if everyone else at table is more stimulating. Everyone should sit up straight, with elbows never touching the table, and lips closed while eating. The way to excellent table manners is for no one to notice you eating.

If you are sitting at a large and formal table, you may begin eating when those on either side of you are served, but when at a smaller table, or informal meal, you must wait to eat. As the hostess lifts her fork, you begin. Of course, if she asks you to

begin eating beforehand, do so. As a guest, it is perfectly acceptable to offer around bread, vegetables or a sauce, and pour water, but don't pour wine unless you are asked to help.

If you are having difficulty knowing how the food should be eaten, watch your hostess, or ask your neighbour. When you are unable to eat anything, eat what you can and discreetly leave the rest. Your hostess should not feel obliged to leave the table to prepare you something else. If you are vegetarian or have religious restrictions on the food that you eat, then say so when writing your acceptance.

A few days after your meal, send a thank-you note to the hostess. For more informal meals or if you have been dining with a friend, a telephone call will be perfectly sufficient to say thank you.

A beautifully laid tale is a most welcoming sight for any guest.

The Envelope Napkin

This is such a charming napkin when it is folded up. I have used it on the breakfast tray for
Mother's Day on page 23.

1 Take a square napkin and fold it in half diagonally to
make a triangle. Lie it flat with the folded edge nearest
you and then fold the left point two-thirds along the
folded edge.

2 Fold the right point across the already folded left side.

3 To form the 'seal', refold the right point back on itself.
Lift the point up towards the centre of the envelope and
press down to make a diamond shape.

4 Fold down the flap and tuck it into the diamond to
seal the envelope.

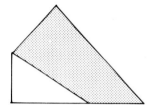 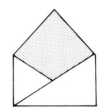 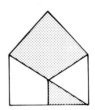 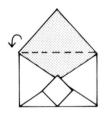

The Fan Napkin

This napkin stands up very well so use it to adorn each table setting. It is featured in Harvest
Thanksgiving on pages 74-6.

1 Take a square napkin and fold the top and bottom
sides together to meet in the middle.

2 Fold it in half again with the outside edges facing
inwards.

3 Now fold it up like an accordion, making four identi-
cal folds.

4 With the folded edge nearest to you, hold the fan
firmly. Fan out the top and press down the front edge of
each valley fold towards the centre front.

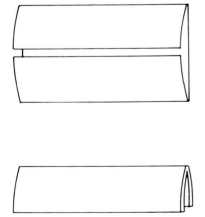 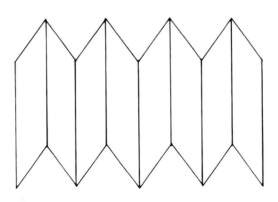 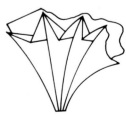

The Dinner Jacket

To finish off these three beautifully folded napkins, here is the one that I used for the Christmas table setting on pages 82-7.

1 Fold a square napkin in half diagonally and then fold over 1.25cm (¹/₂in) of the folded edge to the back. This will ultimately make the collar on the dinner jacket.

2 With the folded edge furthest away from you, take the left point and bring it down to the bottom point. Repeat with the right side.

3 Fold each side point back so that the jacket looks as though its arms are behind its back.

4 Fold back the bottom in the same way.

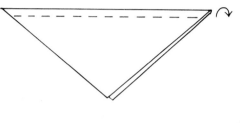

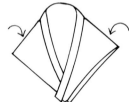

Suppliers

DALER-ROWNEY

Bracknell
Berkshire
RG12 8ST
Telephone: 01344 424621
Fax: 01344 486511

(Working with these exceptionally high-quality products always gives the best results. The papers are versatile and sumptuous, the brushes hard-wearing and subtle. I use many of the products from the lightest tissue paper to thickest paint.)

DMC CREATIVE WORLD

62 Pullman Road
Wigston
Leicester
LE18 2DY
Telephone: 01533 811040

(With 350 colours to choose from in pearl cotton, stranded cotton and sewing cottons, wonderful linens, counted weaves and textures, it is difficult to choose what to use. A full and comprehensive catalogue is available together with a colour sample chart giving the strand textures. All DMC products are fully washable and colour-fast; I for one have tested them.)

PRICE'S PATENT CANDLES

110 York Road
Battersea
London SW11 3RU
Telephone: 0171 228 3345
Fax: 0171 738 0197

(For an exceptional range of candles in all shapes and sizes, textures and colours, Price's candles are available in varying lengths and tapered and straight, thick and thin. These candles are a joy to burn, and are non-drip which is ideal for using with paper shades. They are available at department stores.)

THE LINEN MERCHANT

11 Montpelier Street
London SW7 1EX
Telephone: 0171 584 3654
Fax: 0171 584 3671

(This attractive corner shop is full of the most excellent and varied linens. Every shelf reveals more treasures. Not only is the choice of linens splendid, but the Linen Merchant will personalize with embroidery, and offers expert advice on special requests. This is a modern version of an old-fashioned shop with all the courtesy, individuality, and variety and diversity of stock.)

MANUEL CANOVAS FABRICS

2 North Terrace
Brompton Road
London SW3 2BA
Telephone: 0171 225 2298
Fax: 0171 823 7848

(On sitting at a table for at least two hours, one does have the opportunity of examining the tablecloth very closely. The fabrics at Manuel Canovas are exquisite, they could only enhance any conversation.)

VV ROULEAUX RIBBONS AND BRAIDS

10 Symons Street
Sloane Square
London SW3 2TJ
Telephone: 0171 730 4413
Fax: 0171 730 3468

(An exceptional selection of ribbons, braids, cords, tassels and other numerous trimmings. Their products are also available throughout the country at Liberty shops or via their comprehensive mail order service.)

Index